GREE

Ga

Wildlife

OF BRITAIN AND EUROPE

Garden Wildlife

OF BRITAIN AND EUROPE

bob gibbons
ILLUSTRATED BY john davis

NEW
HOLLAND

This edition published in 2008 by
New Holland Publishers (UK) Ltd

Garfield House, 86-88 Edgware Road, London W2 2EA

80 McKenzie Street, Cape Town 8001, South Africa

Unit 1, 66 Gibbes Street, Chatswood, NSW 2067, Australia

218 Lake Road, Northcote, Auckland, New Zealand

www.newhollandpublishers.com

14 16 18 20 19 17 15 13

ISBN 978 1 85974 929 6

Phototypeset by AKM Associates (UK) Ltd
Reproduction by Scantrans Pte Ltd
Printed and bound in India by
Replika Press Pvt Ltd

Contents

Introduction

This book is a straightforward guide to 150 of the commonest species of animals likely to be seen in gardens; it does not cover plants, either cultivated or wild. Although many more than 150 species are likely to occur in any garden, concentrating on those you will most probably encounter has greatly increased the usefulness of the book. Greater prominence has also been given to the lesser-known invertebrates, on the basis that information about them is harder to come by.

The guide is simple to use, with a study of the illustrations providing the first line of approach when an attempt is being made to identify something new; a check of the descriptions, to ensure that factors such as the distribution match correctly, will help to confirm details. If you are uncertain where to look in the book, a brief outline of the groups covered is given at the end of the introductory sections. Wherever possible, have the book to hand when trying to identify something; it is surprisingly easy to forget details when looking something up later on. One of the great advantages of looking at wildlife in the garden is that you can always have the appropriate books readily to hand, and there is often a second chance if you do not get a good view of something the first time.

The symbols which appear on the illustrations indicate the sexes.

♂ Male
♀ Female

The Ecology of the Garden

Gardens are unlike any single natural habitat, though they share features with most of them. The two key features of the average garden are its great diversity within a small space — no piece of countryside is as varied — and the amount of shelter, coupled, often, with additional food supplies over and above what is naturally available.

Structurally, gardens contain many elements, with trees, shrubs, open grassland (the lawn), bare soil, semi-open flower beds, paved areas, compost heaps, wood-piles, sheds, walls, greenhouses, and often open water in the form of a pond. The soil may be made more varied by the addition of peat, lime, or manure, and some areas may be artificially drier or wetter, such as in a raised bed. Coupled with this diversity of structure, there is an enormous diversity of plants: there are those occurring naturally, often described as weeds, together with all the vegetables, fruit bushes, herbaceous plants, annuals, window-box plants, shrubs and specimen trees, which can collectively amount to hundreds of different species. What is more, they are often selected to have flowers at most times of year, so that the flowering period lasts much longer than in a wild habitat, providing food for insects over a much longer period. Gardens are also more intensively managed than most areas of countryside, which can have beneficial side-effects such as a constant supply of new foliage from shrubs after pruning or cutting.

Despite these differences from more natural countryside, the garden still operates to some extent as an ecosystem, with species all interacting together, though of course any one garden also interacts closely with the gardens or other areas that surround it.

The basis of the system is the plants. Many insects feed directly on plants at some part of their life-cycle; these, in turn provide prey for other insects; and at some point in their development both predators and prey may be eaten by birds. Many birds are also directly dependent on plants, requiring seeds for all or part of their life. Amongst the mammals, there are those, such as mice or squirrels, that feed directly on plant material and others that feed on animals that are themselves dependent on plants. So, one way and another, it all comes down to plants. A garden managed with wildlife in mind could well have many hundreds of different species of animals, all interacting with each other in different ways.

Of the birds that visit any garden, some will be in the country only for the winter. They will be interested in any appropriate food

Introduction

sources, including artificial ones, and they make use of sheltered places to roost in. Natural foods available to them will include seeds from garden plants, and any remnants of crop fruits, such as fallen apples. Some species come primarily for insect food, such as worms and other invertebrates from the lawn and flower beds, or for whatever flying insects they can find. Many will also come to take food put out especially, such as peanuts, seeds, bacon-rind and so on. It is believed that the widespread habit of feeding birds in winter has helped to raise the populations of some commoner birds, such as Blue Tits, and enabled other species to winter further north than they used to. Blackcaps, for example, now winter regularly in Britain, and much of their winter food is made up of artificial supplies. Siskins now regularly move into gardens in late winter, when their natural food sources such as alder seeds have become depleted; without the peanuts, they would be much more likely to die in a cold spell towards the end of winter.

Birds that are resident, or visit only for the summer, may also nest in gardens. For this, they need suitable nest-sites, which may include hedges, shrubberies, old apple trees, shrubs growing against house walls, holes in walls and, of course, nest-boxes. Some species, such as birds of prey, are never really likely to breed in the average garden, but many smaller birds can find somewhere to their liking. When they do nest, they not only require a safe, well-hidden site, but they also need an area of territory from which to draw food to feed their young. This is likely to be a much greater area than one garden alone, and the more suitable habitat there is in the area, the higher the density of birds that can nest there. Most garden birds feed their young on caterpillars and other insects, so the area has to be rich in different plants, which support a corresponding range of insects. In this respect, plants native to the area are generally the most productive, since higher numbers of insects can feed on them.

Mammals will use gardens as food sources, shelter and as breeding sites. Larger mammals, such as Foxes and Badgers, will have a very wide 'home range' within which they will travel and search for food. They could, for example, be based in countryside close to a town, and regularly visit a number of urban gardens to find food. Equally, they could be based in a suitable area of rougher habitat within the urban area, such as a railway bank, waste ground, or even a larger garden. Smaller mammals, such as Hedgehogs or mice, may often live entirely in garden areas, with a home base in one garden and a feeding area that extends over several. To some extent, mammals may change their feeding area according to season, with minor migrations, but not on the same scale as birds.

Amphibians and reptiles behave in a similar way to smaller mammals, moving over a relatively small area. In the case of amphibians, such as frogs and toads, they need to return annually to a breeding site in spring, and this may or may not be in a garden. Toads tend to have large 'ancestral' breeding sites, and it is a matter of chance whether your garden is near enough to one for it to be regularly visited by toads.

It is probably the invertebrates that have the most complicated and demanding life-cycles. There are potentially thousands of different species of insects and other invertebrates that could occur in a garden. Which ones do appear will depend on general features such as climate, proximity of wild areas, pollution levels and, to some extent, chance. But it also depends on whether the garden can provide the features that each species needs. One example may serve to illustrate this complexity. The little Holly Blue butterfly is a

Introduction

common garden visitor. In spring, the female butterflies need to lay their eggs on Holly flowers, because the developing caterpillars eat the young berries. Hollies come in male and female forms, of which the males have flowers but no fruit, so only the females are suitable (in fact, the butterflies not infrequently make a mistake, and lay their eggs on male plants — these are doomed to failure). The caterpillars that have fed successfully on the berries will eventually pupate, and seek out some crevice or other suitable area. When these emerge, through July and August, they need a supply of nectar on which to feed (for example, Bramble blossom) and, after mating, somewhere to lay their eggs. This second generation of the butterfly does not choose Holly, as there would be no developing fruits, but instead chooses Ivy, which comes into flower in late summer and produces fruit through the autumn. The second-generation caterpillars feed on the Ivy flowers and fruits, and will eventually pupate, to spend the winter as pupae, well protected from frost and predators.

Most other insects have equally complex requirements in that they need one or more foodplants for their larvae (caterpillars), a source of nectar from flowers when they are adult, shelter from cold winds, somewhere safe to pass the winter, and so on. A garden designed with wildlife in mind can easily provide all these requirements, for a whole range of insects. The more insects you cater for, the more you will attract birds and mammals to feed on them.

Looking at Wildlife in the Garden

There is nowhere easier to look at wildlife than in the garden. There are so many advantages: you can be there throughout all the seasons, watching for birds to nest or particular nectar flowers to come out; you can be out early in the morning, to hear birds singing, or find roosting butterflies; and you can keep an eye on all the changes that take place, looking again at species you are unsure of. And, best of all, you can alter the characteristics of the garden to increase the amount of wildlife that you have.

Birds are ever-popular subjects for study and photography. If possible, try to arrange to have a feeding area close to a window from which you can regularly watch. In this way, you can quickly discover and identify any species that come to the garden for food. Similarly, bird-baths and even nest-boxes can be placed somewhere visible, though it is good idea to have some further from the house, too, for the less brave species. A pair of binoculars is always useful, preferably kept somewhere accessible for instant use, to allow closer views of unusual birds, or even the occasional mammal, butterfly or dragonfly that you cannot get close enough to. They can even be helpful in very poor light if, for example, you are fortunate enough to have visiting nocturnal mammals.

During the breeding season, roughly April to June, the male birds of each pair will spend a good deal of time singing. For most species, this is done most openly and frequently early in the morning (hence the term 'dawn chorus'). As the garden is, literally, on the doorstep, it is well worth going out on calm dry mornings, as soon after dawn as possible, to observe which birds are singing, and how many there are of each. If so inclined, you can plot their whereabouts on a plan of the garden, and roughly estimate the number of pairs you have of each species, and what their territory covers. If your garden is only small then it will just form a part of a territory, but you will usually be able to see where else they are singing, in other gardens. You can also use your observations to guess where the birds are nesting; this is most easily done when they are feeding the young, as the adults inevitably have to keep returning to the same place carrying food, and you will only need to watch for a while to figure out where the nest is. After observing a nest, make sure that it is still well-hidden after you leave, or predators such as Magpies will quickly find it.

If you are interested to know what insects visit your garden, it is always worth going out at night with a torch. Many insects, and other invertebrates, are strongly nocturnal and are much more likely to be seen at night. Look closely at flowers, to see moths,

Introduction

earwigs and other creatures feeding on them. The ground may have ground beetles, centipedes, woodlice and others, and you may also discover that you have more slugs and snails than you thought. If you have a pond, check this for different insects, and also for newts, which tend to be most active at night-time, especially during the breeding season. Nocturnal forays may also reveal the presence of Hedgehogs, or the possibility of larger visitors such as Foxes, that you were hitherto unaware of. You may hear the calls of hunting bats, or the squeak of mice or shrews (though usually only younger people have acute enough hearing to pick up these high-pitched sounds).

To extend your knowledge of the nocturnal insect visitors further, a moth-trap can prove useful. These traps are strong sources of light, usually using a mercury-vapour lamp, together with some form of box into which moths and other insects drawn to the light can fall but not readily escape. They can be bought or made easily. The information that they reveal can be remarkable; if you simply observe your garden by day, you may see perhaps half a dozen species of moths in a year. People who set light-traps, and record them regularly, not infrequently catch 300 to 400 different species of moths, together with a range of different insects. Specimens should always be released after observation.

If you have a pond — and every good wildlife garden should have one — then it is fascinating to take a closer look at the wildlife in it. It is rewarding to spend some time on a warm sunny day simply looking at the surface and under the water, just to see what goes on there. There is an amazing amount of life in a good pond, but most of it is rarely seen since creatures behave differently when they think they are being watched. If you can spend half an hour or so watching whilst remaining still, then much more will be revealed

Dragonflies or damselflies may be emerging, mud-flies may perform their intriguing wing-waving courtship behaviour, frogs may come to the surface to sunbathe, and predatory beetle larvae may catch their prey, to mention just a few possibilities. Further opportunities for observation can be gained by having a reasonably large aquarium in the house, ready set-up and stabilised, into which you can bring tadpoles or other aquatic creatures to watch them for a few days before returning them to the pond. If the aquarium is large enough, it is even possible to bring in larger creatures such as newts, for example, to see them during their breeding season.

Finally, keeping a notebook of what you see is particularly useful if you are developing the garden for wildlife, as you can look back over the years to see what you have achieved. Even as a simple record it will be interesting, as you can add up the total numbers of birds that visit, check when you first saw a butterfly in previous years, or make notes to help with later identification.

Making a Garden for Wildlife

A logical extension of an interest in wildlife, if you have a garden, is to think about ways in which you can attract more wildlife into it. This serves two main functions: first, you perform a useful conservation function, as more and more countryside is lost under the plough or under buildings. Your own garden can become an oasis, free from pesticides and full of life. Secondly, you can give yourself and any visitors great pleasure by increasing the amount of wildlife there is to be seen.

There many ways in which a garden can be improved for wildlife, which vary according to its size and situation, and according to how much time and money you wish to put into it, or what proportion of the garden you wish to devote to wildlife. It need not mean that the garden looks untidy, nor does it mean that you cannot grow normal flowers, fruit and vegetables. A combination of more wildlife together with normal garden requirements is perfectly possible. There is not space here to go into full details of how to make a really successful wildlife garden, but some of the general ideas are discussed, and books recommended in the bibliography can help with further information.

There are a number of good general principles, that can be applied in any garden, which will help to increase the range of animals that visit. First, cut down on pesticides of all types. Some pesticides may be required for your particular form of gardening, but try to keep them to the absolute minimum. They are harmful to many insects, and can also reduce the number of birds and mammals that visit, or they can harm those that do. We have enough pesticides in the countryside and in the food we eat, without adding unnecessarily to the quantity. It may mean that you have to adopt some other methods of control if you grow vegetables, but there are many other possibilities available.

Second, aim to have as wide a range of plants in your garden as possible. Grow species that flower at all seasons, and include a range of plants that produce nectar for bees, butterflies and other insects. A small list of such plants is provided below, and books and specialist nurseries can recommend others. If possible, include the caterpillar foodplants of some of the commoner butterflies (these are given under the individual species), so that they have the possibility of breeding. Also consider plants that produce seeds or fruits which birds will eat, such as Teasels, Cotoneaster species, Hawthorn, Ivy, Rowan and many others. In general, even if you are not sure what each species achieves, aim for variety in your planting

— it is bound to produce an increase in the range of wildlife, and you may discover some surprising favourites amongst the plants you put in. With trees and shrubs, it is worth planting, or keeping, a high proportion of species that are native to your area. A good flora can be consulted if you are uncertain which species are native locally; for most areas, such plants as Hawthorn, Blackthorn, Crab-apple, Guelder Rose, Dog-rose, Willows, Honeysuckle, Rowan and Birch will be highly suitable. These native trees and shrubs will support a much wider range of insects than exotic plants would.

Some suggested nectar-bearing plants

Apple Mint	*Mentha* × *rotundifolia*
Blackthorn	*Prunus spinosus*
	Buddleia davidii
	Caryopteris × *clandonensis*
Cuckoo Flower	*Cardamine pratensis*
Dame's Violet	*Hesperis matronalis*
Globe Thistle	*Echinops ritro*
Hawthorn	*Crataegus monogyna*
	Hebe spp
Hemp Agrimony	*Eupatorium cannabinum*
Honeysuckle	*Lonicera periclymenum*
Hyssop	*Hyssopus officinalis*
Ice-plant	*Sedum spectabile*
Marjoram	*Origanum vulgare*
Michaelmas Daisies	*Aster* spp.
Sweet William	*Dianthus barbatus*

Although the garden may need to look generally tidy, a little less order in certain aspects of it will be appreciated by wildlife. For example, if more dead seed-heads are left on through the winter, they may not only be food for birds but they may provide hibernation sites for insects and food for other creatures. Lawns can be cut a little less tightly, and not fertilised or herbicided, so that they can become more flowery, with more food for birds, more resident insects and more nectar for visiting insects. Although a lawn that is not smooth and green may not appeal at first, it can soon become acceptable and it can perform all the functions of a

Introduction

normal lawn, while being more attractive and better for wildlife. Finally, a few weeds here and there, perhaps in places where they are not so likely to spread, can undoubtedly be a good thing, as they provide seeds and herbage for many creatures to feed on, and cover for others to hide under.

In general, it is a good idea to put food out in the garden, especially for birds. There are few hard and fast rules, but most people prefer to put food out from late autumn until about April; for the rest of the year, birds will find plenty for themselves, and they are more likely to take the correct natural food for their nestlings. There are many types of food that can be put out, depending on what birds occur in your area, how much time and money you want to spend, and what scraps you happen to have. A good combination includes one or more peanut dispensers, a bird-table offering a proprietary bird-food mixture, and a selection of other foods as and when

available. For example, cheese, raisins, bacon-rind and other scraps will all be popular. 'Semi-natural' foods such as apples, a head of sunflower seeds, or other fruits will all go down well. If you have apple trees, it is possible to keep the apples in storage, then bring them out through the winter to maintain a steady supply until you run out or they go rotten. You can also buy imported apples, which will be greatly appreciated by Blackbirds, visiting Thrushes of various sorts, and Blackcaps. Attaching one or more of the fruits to a table and spreading others on a lawn will attract a wider range of birds. You can also try putting fatty substances into crevices, to attract Woodpeckers or Nuthatches, if they are in the area.

These are all good general principles to follow if you want more wildlife in the garden. However, if you wish to go into it more deeply, it is worth considering the possibility of making various habitats in the garden, with wildlife specifically in mind. Possibilities include a pond, a meadow area, a 'woodland edge', and a butterfly border, all on a small scale. There is not space in this book to look at all of these in detail, but a pond and a butterfly border are considered more closely below.

A good pond is the focal point of a wildlife garden. It acts as a place where birds and mammals can drink and feed, where amphibians breed, feed and sunbathe, and where numerous insects can live or visit. If well sited and well designed, it is likely to be seething with life.

Size is not too important, though usually the larger it is the better. However, even a very small pond, only 1 metre or so across, can serve many of the functions of a larger pond. Profile, however, *is* important. The pond should have at least one side that slopes gently from the edge to the deepest point, while other areas should have a ledge or two on which plants can be placed. If possible, there should be a minimum depth of about 50cm, though this is not exactly critical. The pond should be sited where it receives plenty of sunshine, and as far as possible it should not receive quantities of leaves from nearby trees in autumn – if there are trees nearby, site the pond up the prevailing wind, if this is possible. Shaded or leaf-filled ponds have very little life, as the water becomes de-oxygenated. It is also a good idea to site the pond next to some other rough habitat, at least on one side, so that amphibians and other creatures can approach and leave the pond under cover.

When siting and construction are complete, there are two other points to bear in mind. First, there should be a good range of plants

Introduction

in the pond, to include erect emergent aquatics, such as Flowering Rush, Arrowhead, or others, together with oxygenating plants such as Canadian Pondweed or Water Crowfoot, and a few floating-leaved plants such as Frog-bit, Water-lilies and some Water-crowfoot species. This mixture helps to oxgenate the pond water, shades some parts from the sun, provides cover from predators for invertebrates, and offers structures for species such as dragonflies and damselflies to emerge onto.

Second, it is best to avoid stocking the pond with fish if you want to retain a lot of wildlife. It is possible for both to co-exist, but fish certainly keep the number of insects such as dragonflies down, and if the pond is poorly vegetated their effect will be very marked.

A 'butterfly border' can be a very attractive feature, as well as being somewhere that brings in butterflies and other insects. The basic principles of a good butterfly border are to provide a wide range of nectar-bearing plants and foodplants, somewhere warm and sheltered. To enhance the effect, there should be masses of suitable plants together, so that insects can see or scent the flowers from a distance.

Unless you already have an appropriately placed hedge or shrub area, you need to create an initial framework of suitable shrubs that will be at the back of the border, on its north side. These could include such species as the famous Butterfly Bush *Buddleia davidii*, other species of *Buddleia* such as *B. globosa*, or attractive flowery shrubs such as Guelder Rose. If possible, plant them in a crescent, with the two arms curling round towards the south. Within this crescent-shaped framework, you then need to plant masses of nectar-bearing flowers, working downwards in size, with the smallest flowers at the front. For example, just in front of the shrub framework, one might plant *Hebe* species, such as *H. albicans* or *H. brachysiphon*, Hemp Agrimony, Ice-plant *Sedum spectabile*, larger Michaelmas Daisies, and other medium-size plants. In front of these, the mixture could include Sweet Williams, Pinks, dwarf Michaelmas Daisies, Red Valerian, Fleabane, *Caryopteris* × *clandonensis*, Bugle and Marjoram, amongst others, aiming for a variety of flowering times.

As it matures, this border will attract more and more butterflies and other insects. It will be useful to keep records of which species are most successful in attracting the insects; different varieties and even strains of flowers can be successful to a greater or lesser degree, and if you find that some of the plants are achieving nothing, they can always be replaced. Incidentally, it will also be worth checking the butterfly border at dusk and in the night, especially if you have planted night-scented species like Honeysuckle or *Nicotiana* species, because it will also attract many moths and other nocturnal insects.

Other small-scale habitats that can be created, if you have the space and time, include a woodland edge, with small trees fronted by shrubs and underplanted with woodland flowers; a flowery meadow area, bright with Ox-eye daisy, Red Clover, Self-heal, Knapweed, Sorrel, Cowslips, and whatever else suits your soil; and a boggy area, possibly next to the pond, formed by using a pond liner but filling the depression with soil and planting up with marsh plants such as Marsh Marigolds, Hairy Willowherb, or sedges. All of these complement each other, and broaden the range of wildlife that your garden will attract.

The Groups of Garden Invertebrates

It is assumed that users of this book can readily distinguish the various vertebrate groups, such as mammals, birds and amphibians from each other. However, the multiplicity of invertebrate groups may pose more of a problem. Invertebrates are animals without backbones, and they include the vast range of insects, together with such non-insect invertebrates as spiders, centipedes and others. The following is a very brief guide to some of the main groups.

Insects

Most insects have wings and 6 legs, though there is much variation within this pattern. Damselflies and Dragonflies (pp 44 to 45) are large long-bodied predatory insects, with 2 pairs of usually translucent wings, and short antennae. Dragonflies are larger and stronger, and perch with their wings held out at right angles; damselflies have a more fluttery flight, and usually perch with their wings held along the body. Butterflies and moths (pp 46 to 59) are very familiar as a group; there are no hard and fast distinctions between the two groups, but as a general rule butterflies are day-flying, have clubbed antennae, and hold their wings vertically above the body when at rest; moths are mainly nocturnal, have feathery or unclubbed antennae, and do not hold their wings vertically. Grasshoppers and Crickets (pp 60 to 62) are bulky insects, most of which have greatly enlarged legs for jumping; most species have rather poorly developed wings. Males of most species sing in some way. Grasshoppers have short antennae, while Bush-crickets have very long antennae and the females have dagger-like ovipositors.

Introduction

Amongst the remaining insects, the Bugs (pp 63 to 68) are a huge group which all have two pairs of wings and piercing, needle-like mouthparts, designed for sucking. The Flies (pp 69 to 77) are characterised by having only one pair of wings, with the second pair being reduced to small balancing organs. The Hymenopterans (pp 78 to 83) include ants, wasps and bees: the winged species all have 2 pairs of wings, and all species have a marked waist and, usually, biting mouthparts. Beetles (pp 84 to 89) are generally familiar in form, due to the characteristic hardened front wings, which form a cover, known as the elytra, under which the membranous rear wings are folded; in most species, this elytra covers most of the body.

Other invertebrates

Other invertebrates have a wide variety of forms. The Molluscs (pp 92 to 93), which include slugs and snails, have amorphous slimy bodies and an external shell (in the case of snails), or a much-reduced shell (in the case of slugs); they are hermaphrodite. The Spiders (pp 94 to 95) have 8 legs, a distinctly 3-part body, and the ability to spin webs. Harvestmen (p 96) are similar, but the body is undivided, they cannot produce webs, and they are less aggressively predatory.

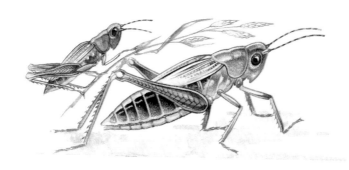

Mammals

Hedgehog *Erinaceus europaeus*
Unmistakable small-medium mammal with a body length of 22-29cm and an almost complete covering of long spines on its back. These spines are brown tipped with white and the fur below is rather paler. The nose is pointed. Although it occurs in many habitats, especially woodland, the Hedgehog is a regular visitor to gardens for food and may become resident. It feeds on numerous invertebrates, including slugs, but will also take scraps, milk and other artificial foods. It hibernates through most of the winter, often under leaves. Common and widespread almost throughout the area.

Badger *Meles meles* Very distinctive largish mammal with a total body and tail length of up to 1m, though usually less. The longitudinally striped black and white face immediately distinguishes the species; the rest of the coat is a rather variable mixture of black and grey. Lives in underground burrows known as 'setts', which may become very large and have several entrances; these are only rarely located in gardens, but the animal frequently visits to pass through or to find food. It is almost entirely nocturnal, returning to the sett during the day. Common and widespread throughout the area.

Red Fox *Vulpes vulpes* Dog-like, medium-sized mammal with a total length of up to 75cm. The appearance is distinctive, with pointed ears, sharp muzzle, long bushy tail, and lovely reddish fur with white on the breast. The range of calls, from wailing to barking, often indicates a fox's presence before it is seen. Although mainly nocturnal, it will quite often move around in daylight or sunbathe. A scavenger, it will readily visit gardens in search of scraps. A very common and widespread species.

Mole *Talpa europaea* A smallish mammal with a body length of 10–16cm. The fur is velvety black, and males and females are very similar. The animal is highly adapted to underground life, with short strong legs and flat feet, enabling it to dig very rapidly. Although rarely seen, its effects are much more conspicuous; the molehills that not infrequently appear on lawns are the soil that is removed at regular intervals as a tunnel is excavated. Moles are common and widespread throughout most of northern Europe, but replaced in southern Europe by the closely related Mediterranean Mole *Talpa occidentalis*.

Mammals

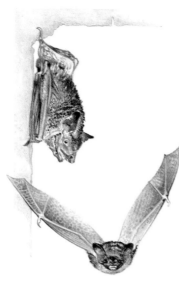

Pipistrelle Bat *Pipistrellus pipistrellus* Very small bat with a body length of only 3.5–4.5cm. Males and females are similar, with variable dark brownish fur, sometimes tinged orange, and lighter underparts. The ears are about 1cm long. Frequently roosts, and sometimes breeds, in loft spaces or other sheltered situations around houses, and can often be seen emerging just after sunset and flying around houses or over gardens. The species is common and widespread virtually throughout Europe, and is the most frequently seen bat in most areas.

Long-eared Bats *Plecotus auritus* and *P. austriacus* Two very similar species, only relatively recently separated as distinct. They have a body length of 3.7–4.8cm with conspicuous ears that are 3–4cm long. The fur is light brown above, paler below, though the rarer species *P. austriacus* tends to be greyer, with a darker face. Although widespread in natural habitats, they regularly use houses as roosts. They emerge just after sunset to feed on insects, when their long ears may be visible before the light fades. One or other species may be found throughout the area, except in the far north.

Grey Squirrel *Sciurus carolinensis* Very similar in overall size and shape to the Red Squirrel. The coat is essentially grey, with white underparts; however, in summer a reddish tinge develops, more so in some individuals than others, though never the rich hue of the Red Squirrel; the Grey's lack of ear-tufts also distinguishes the species. A regular garden visitor, it soon learns to feed from nut dispensers and other feeders, often becoming tame. Introduced from North America, it is now abundant throughout southern Britain, still spreading, and occasionally found on mainland Europe.

Red Squirrel *Sciurus vulgaris* A familiar species. The head and body total about 20–25cm in length, with the tail adding a further 15–20cm. The coat is a rich reddish-brown, with a white underside; reddish ear-tufts are especially prominent in winter. Builds domed nests, known as 'dreys', usually in conifers, and feeds mainly on pine cones. In areas where the species is common, it frequently visits gardens for scraps, sometimes becoming quite tame. Widespread throughout mainland Europe, though in Britain it is mainly confined to northern regions, with a few southern outposts.

Mammals

House Mouse *Mus musculus*
A small mammal with a body length of 7-9cm and a long tail. The fur is dull greyish-brown, usually only slightly paler below. The squeaking call is commonly heard. Abundant everywhere, particularly near habitation, often living within a house, or under garden sheds. Although mainly nocturnal, this mouse can occasionally be seen in the day, and its droppings and musty odour often betray its presence. Feeds on seeds, cheese and scraps, quickly finding domestic food. Widespread virtually throughout Europe.

Wood Mouse *Apodemus sylvaticus* Also known as the Long-tailed Field Mouse, this small mammal is distinctly larger than the House Mouse, with a body length of 8-13cm and a long thin tail. The fur is brown on the flanks, yellow on the sides and pale grey below. Although it is most common in rough woodland and grassy places, it regularly occurs in larger gardens, or where there is suitable habitat nearby. It will come to food, though is less adaptable than the House Mouse in this respect. Widespread virtually throughout Europe.

Field Vole *Microtus agrestis*
A small mammal with a body length of 9–12cm and a tail of 3–5cm. Similar in appearance to mice, but generally has a rounder blunter face, shorter ears and a shorter tail. The coat is greyish-brown above, more pure grey below. Squeaks frequently and noisily. It is very abundant in rough grassy areas, and will frequently occur in gardens in suitable places, especially if there is good habitat nearby. Feeds mainly on grasses and other leaves, and does not normally come for domestic scraps. Widespread and common throughout, except the far south of Europe.

Brown Rat *Rattus norvegicus*
Medium-small mammal, with a body length of up to 28cm and a longish thick scaly tail. The fur is shaggy, greyish-brown, often paler below, but variable in colour. Although similar in form to mice, the Brown Rat's larger size distinguishes the species. Frequently occurs around houses and gardens, where it soon finds scraps or bird-food, though generally unpopular and rarely tolerated for long. Common around built-up areas almost everywhere, throughout the world.

Mammals/Birds

Common Shrew *Sorex araneus*
Very small mammal with a
body length of 6-8cm and a tail
about half as long again.
Although superficially similar
to mice, it is unrelated. The
coat is usually dark brown
above and paler below, though
variable according to age and
season. The nose is thin,
pointed and whiskery. Feeds
almost entirely on
invertebrates such as worms
and woodlice, and does not
come for scraps, though
frequently occurs around
gardens and not uncommonly
falls victim to domestic cats.
Occurs throughout Europe,
except in the far south.

Black-headed Gull *Larus
ridibundus* A rather small gull,
35-40cm long. Adult
essentially white, with greyish
wings tipped black; in
summer, it has a deep
chocolate-brown hood, a red
bill and red legs; in winter, the
hood is reduced to just a spot
behind the eye, and the legs
and bill are less bright. These
gulls regularly visit gardens
for food, often in noisy groups
attracted to scraps. Abundant
throughout the year in much
of Europe, though in the far
north a summer visitor only,
and in the far south mainly a
winter visitor.

Pied Wagtail *Motacilla alba*
Characteristic wagtail, with a body length of 17–18cm and the typical long tail which is frequently flicked. It has attractive pied plumage, with a black back, top of the head and chin, though continental birds (known as White Wagtails) have paler backs, and the female Pied Wagtail has an intermediate slate-grey back. The 'chis-sick' call is distinctive. A common garden resident and visitor, nesting in Ivy, or holes in walls, and frequently feeding on lawns, though rarely visiting bird-tables as it is insectivorous. Common throughout Europe, resident all year in milder areas.

Collared Dove *Streptopelia decaocto* A small dove with a body length of about 28–32cm. Both sexes are similar, with a buff back, pale pinkish-grey head and chest, and a distinctive black half-collar, edged with white. The call, 'coo-cooo-coo', can become very monotonous. Nests in trees around gardens and farmyards, and frequently visits bird-tables to feed. The species has spread dramatically northwards and westwards through Europe during this century, and is common throughout the area except in the far north and in Spain.

Birds

Woodpigeon *Columba palumbus*
The largest of the pigeons,
with a body length of about
40cm. The plumage is
essentially grey and both
sexes are similar, with a
pinkish breast, white wing-
bars and a white neck-bar
edged with green. The call is a
monotonous and familiar 'coo-
coo-coo, cu-coo', repeated
endlessly during the breeding
season. An abundant species
all year over most of Europe,
except the far north, breeding
in trees and regularly visiting
gardens, where it may raid
fruit and crops, as well as
visiting bird-tables.

Tawny Owl *Strix aluco* A
medium-sized owl with a body
length of 36–40cm. The sexes
are similar, both having
brown plumage, mottled and
streaked, darker on the back
than on the breast; the face is
round and greyish. The call is
the familiar 'tu-whit-tu-
whoo', combined with a
harsher 'kee-wick' at times.
Although essentially a
woodland bird, it is common
in gardens with trees nearby,
and the young birds may
often be heard calling at night
in summer. Feeds on mice,
voles, small birds and larger
insects. Common throughout
except in the far north.

Great Spotted Woodpecker
Dendrocopos major Boldly
marked medium-sized bird
with a body length of 22–24cm.
The adult plumage is black
and white, with a red area
under the tail; the male has a
red patch at the back of the
neck where the female is all
black. Young birds have a red
crown. Both sexes produce a
far-carrying sound by
drumming on trees in spring
and early summer. Basically a
woodland bird, but regularly
visits gardens for food, both
from old timber and from
fatty scraps. The nest is built
in a tree-cavity. A common
resident throughout Europe,
except Ireland.

Swift *Apus apus* A smallish bird
with a body length of 16–17cm.
Both sexes are all black, apart
from a few paler marks; the
wings are long, narrow and
sickle-shaped, the body
streamlined and the tail
slightly forked. (Distinct from
the unrelated Swallow, which
has white underparts and a
longer tail.) Almost entirely
aerial in habits, only coming
to ground to nest, most
commonly in the roof spaces
of houses. Parties fly at high
speed over towns, screaming
as they go. A common
summer visitor throughout,
except in the far north.

Birds

House Martin *Delichon urbica*
A smallish bird with a body
length of 12-13cm. Male and
female are similar, with
bluish-black plumage above,
apart from a conspicuous
white rump, and silvery-white
plumage below. The shortly
forked tail, together with the
white rump, readily
distinguishes the species from
Swallows. The nests are most
commonly built on house
walls, tight against the eaves,
often in small colonies, and
the birds are very visible as
they visit the nests, feed in
the air, or perch on wires. An
abundant summer visitor
throughout Europe.

Starling *Sturnus vulgaris* A
medium-sized bird with a
body length of 20-23cm. Both
sexes are similar, with glossy
greenish-black plumage that
becomes more heavily
speckled with white in winter;
the bill is bright yellow in
summer, duller in winter. The
song consists of a variety of
wheezy calls. It is an abundant
and conspicuous species, often
nesting around houses, and
regularly visiting lawns and
bird-tables for food. Resident
throughout much of Europe,
except in the far north and
south; in Spain, the resident
equivalent is the darker
unspeckled Spotless Starling.

Black Redstart *Phoenicurus ochruros* A smallish bird with a body length of 13–15cm. The male has a dark charcoal-coloured plumage, with a white wing-flash, while the female is browner. Both sexes have a rusty-red tail. The male sings his brief scratchy warbling song from wires and rooftops throughout the breeding season. A frequent summer visitor (or resident in the far south) to towns throughout most of Europe, except Scandinavia, and still very rare in Britain.

Blackbird *Turdus merula* Very familiar medium-sized bird with a body length of 24–26cm. The male is all black apart from the yellow bill and eye-ring, whilst the female is browner, with a speckled breast and duller yellow bill. The male has a strong melodious song, and both sexes have a familiar alarm chatter. Although common in many habitats, the species is particularly adapted to gardens, where it is abundant. Nests in hedges and shrubs, beginning early in the year, and feeds on almost anything from raspberries to worms. A widespread resident through-out, except in the far north.

Song-Thrush *Turdus philomelos*
A familiar medium-sized bird
with a body length of 22–24cm.
Male and female are similar,
brown above, with a pale
breast strongly spotted with
black, and a yellowish patch
on the throat. The song is
attractive, with the
characteristic habit of
repeating phrases several
times. A particularly common
species in gardens, nesting in
hedges and shrubs, and
feeding on the lawns and
flowerbeds; where snails are
abundant, the Thrush may
use stones as 'anvils' to crack
the shells, leaving the remains
scattered around. Resident or
regular visitor throughout
Europe.

Blue Tit *Parus caeruleus* This
tiny bird has a body length of
11–12cm. Male and female are
similar, the familiar plumage
consisting of yellow breast,
blue crown, white face, and
olive and blue-green back;
there is also a conspicuous
black eyestripe. The call is a
high repeated note. An
abundant species in gardens,
nesting in holes in walls or
trees, or quickly finding
suitable nest-boxes; it comes
readily to nut dispensers,
especially in winter, though
the young are fed mainly on
caterpillars. Common and
resident throughout the area,
except in the far north.

Great Tit *Parus major* Small but striking bird with a body length of 13–15cm. Male and female are similar, with a black head, conspicuous white cheeks and a yellow breast with a strong central black stripe (the black head and breast stripe help to distinguish the species from the Blue Tit). The call notes are very varied, with over 50 types recorded. Common in many habitats, but regularly visiting and nesting in gardens, where it is one of the commonest users of peanut-dispensers. It is widespread throughout most of Europe, resident everywhere except in the far north.

Greenfinch *Carduelis chloris* Stoutly billed medium-small bird with a body length of 14–15cm. The male is basically greenish-yellow, with a yellowish breast and yellow edges to the tail and wings; the female is similar, but paler and duller in colour. Both sexes have thick pale pinkish bills. The call is a nasal 'zwee'. Regularly nests in gardens, in trees and shrubs, as well as visiting to feed, being especially fond of peanuts and other seeds. A common resident over most of Europe, except the far north.

Birds

Serin *Serinus serinus* A small bird with a body length of 11–12cm. Male and female are broadly similar, with streaked brownish backs, yellowish rumps, pale breasts speckled with black, and yellow around the head; the male is generally brighter, and has more yellow on the head and breast. The call is an attractive tinkling 'sizzle' often heard before the bird is seen. Regularly nests in and visits gardens. A frequent summer visitor through most of Europe, though barely reaching Britain or Scandinavia, and resident all year in the south.

Siskin *Carduelis spinus* Small, slender bird with a body length of 11–13cm. Both male and female are greenish-yellow, with white flanks, streaked black; the male tends to be brighter than the female, with more yellow on the throat, and a distinct black crown and bib. The song is best described as 'twittering'. Essentially a woodland bird, but in recent years it has begun to visit gardens regularly from midwinter onwards, feeding mainly on peanuts, as natural food supplies run low. Common and widespread over most of Europe, resident in many areas, but a summer visitor only, in the north.

Chaffinch *Fringilla coelebs*
Small-medium bird with a body length of 14–16cm. The male is brightly coloured, with a pinkish breast and face, grey head, brown back and double white wing-bars; the female is duller, with a pale, slightly pink breast and a greenish-grey back. It has an attractive descending song and a distinctive 'pink-pink' call note. Regularly breeds in or visits gardens, where it readily comes for food, often becoming very tame. An abundant resident bird over most of Europe.

Goldfinch *Carduelis carduelis* An attractive small-medium bird with a body length of 11.5–12.5cm. Male and female are similar, both equally colourful: the face is red with white cheeks, head and nape are black, while the rest of the plumage is a combination of brown, pink, white and black, with conspicuous yellow wing-bars. The song is an attractive tinkling. Has a particular liking for gardens, often nesting in old fruit trees. Feeds on Teasels, Thistles and other seed-heads, including ones especially put out. A common resident over much of Europe.

Birds

Bullfinch *Pyrrhula pyrrhula*
Rather dumpy, small-medium
bird with a body length of 14–
15cm. Male and female are
broadly similar, both having a
black cap, greyish back, black
tail and white rump; the male,
however, has a bright pinkish
breast, while the female has a
duller buff breast. The call is a
soft single note. It is more
secretive than many garden
birds, but frequently breeds in
garden hedges or trees. Feeds
on a variety of buds and seeds,
and has a bad reputation for
its ability to destroy many
fruit-tree buds. Common and
resident almost throughout
Europe.

Robin *Erithacus rubecula* Very
familiar, smallish dumpy bird
with a body length of 13–15cm.
Male and female are identical,
brownish above and pale
below, with a conspicuous red
breast and face; the juvenile is
barred brown, and lacks the
red breast. It has a ticking call
and a thin warbling song. A
characteristic and well-known
garden bird, readily becoming
tame, and feeding from bird-
tables, or on invertebrates
turned up by garden activities
such as digging. Common and
widespread resident
throughout much of Europe,
though a summer visitor only
in Scandinavia.

House Sparrow *Passer domesticus*
Perhaps the most familiar of
all garden birds; smallish, with
a body length of 14-16cm. The
male is attractively marked,
with a black bib and face, a
grey crown, chocolate-brown
nape, mottled brown and grey
back, and a pale underside.
The female is duller and lacks
the head colours. The call is
an insistent 'chirrup'. Almost
always associated with man,
feeding at bird-tables and on
many human by-products; the
nests are built in noisy
colonies, usually around
buildings. An abundant
resident throughout Europe.
The Tree Sparrow *(P.
montanus)* is similar, with a
brown crown and smaller bib,
but is much less frequent.

Magpie *Pica pica* Very
distinctive medium-large bird
with a body length of 42-50cm,
much of which is tail. Male
and female are identical, with
boldly marked glossy black
and white plumage, unlikely
to be mistaken for anything
else. It has a harsh 'chak-chak-
chak' call. Regularly visits
gardens in search of food, and
breeds in untidy domed nests
if there are suitable trees. It is
a scavenger and minor
predator, eating carrion, eggs,
young birds, and almost
everything else. An abundant
resident throughout Europe.

Amphibians

Smooth Newt *Triturus vulgaris*
Also known as the Common Newt, a medium-sized amphibian with a body length of 6-9cm, occasionally more. For most of the year, both male and female have smooth velvety skin, but during the spring breeding season the male becomes crested, and more strongly marked with black blotches and a yellowish belly; the female is duller, and does not become crested. The eggs are laid singly on aquatic plants, hatching into tadpoles. The species often occurs in garden ponds, where it is most visible in the breeding season, especially at night. Common and widespread almost throughout the area.

Common Toad *Bufo bufo*
Familiar plump amphibian, of which the female may reach about 14cm long and the male 9cm. It is very variable in colour, usually grey or blackish-brown above, pale below, and covered with small warts. Toads only rarely breed in gardens, since they prefer larger ponds, but they frequently visit to feed on insects and other invertebrates, — including Slugs and other unwelcome species — and to hibernate. The eggs (spawn) are laid in long double strings, produced in March–April. The species is common and widespread almost throughout northern and central Europe.

Common Frog *Rana temporaria*
A familiar amphibian, with a body length of up to 13cm. Smoother skinned than the Common Toad, it is highly variable in colour, but most commonly greenish-yellow to brown, blotched darker, and with a whitish belly. Frogs hop whereas Toads normally walk. The eggs are laid very early in the year, from January onwards, in jelly-covered masses; the tadpoles take several years to become adults. Frogs will choose almost any water body and will quickly find garden ponds. Predatory on insects, slugs and other invertebrates. A very common and widespread species, in suitable habitats, throughout the area.

Slow-worm *Anguis fragilis* A snake-like legless lizard with a long, narrow cylindrical body up to 50cm long, but usually less. The colour varies from grey-brown to reddish, usually appearing shiny due to the scales covering the body. The male has a uniform colour, whilst the female and young have a black stripe down the back. The Slow-worm feeds on slugs, flies and other invertebrates, and commonly comes into gardens, living in compost heaps, under corrugated iron, or in stony banks. It is quite harmless and welcome as a controller of pests. Common and widespread throughout the area.

Common Lizard *Lacerta vivipara*
A typical smallish lizard with a total length of up to 17cm, though usually less. It is very variable in colour, most commonly brown or grey with numerous dark markings and stripes down the back, and a paler underside. The young are usually born live (rather than as eggs), though eggs may be laid in some southern areas. Lizards are common and widespread throughout in a variety of habitats, and they may enter gardens from nearby habitat, or be resident in larger suitable gardens.

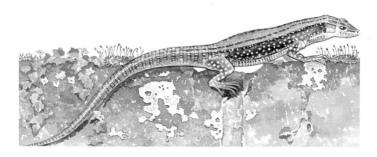

Wall Lizard *Podarcis muralis*
A small-medium lizard with a total body length of up to 20cm, though usually less. The colour is very variable, though usually some shade of brownish-grey mottled and striped with darker and lighter markings. It is similar to the Common Lizard, but tends to have a larger head and legs. It lays eggs, rather than bearing live young, and most commonly lives in holes in walls and banks. This species is virtually absent from Britain, but widespread in Europe and increasingly common southwards.

Grass Snake *Natrix natrix*
Large handsome snake with a body length that regularly reaches 1m, and occasionally 1.5m. It is variable in colour, usually greenish-grey or greenish-brown above, with rows of dots or short stripes down the back; the throat is white or pale yellow, and there is a conspicuous yellowish collar behind the head. The female lays large white eggs, often choosing compost heaps, because they are warm and sheltered; later, tiny snakes emerge, and may be seen in the garden. The Grass Snake is quite harmless. Widespread and quite common, except in the far north.

Adder *Vipera berus* A medium-sized snake with a body length of up to 60cm, occasionally more but usually less. The ground colour is variable, most commonly greyish or brownish, distinctively marked with a strong dark zig-zag pattern all along the back. It lacks the yellow collar of the Grass Snake. Adders are venomous, and should be treated with caution, though it is rare that they actually inflict a serious wound. Common in dry habitats almost throughout the area, visiting larger gardens, or those that have suitable habitat within them.

Damselflies

Large Red Damselfly
Pyrrhosoma nymphula A
medium-sized damselfly,
about 3cm long, mainly red in
colour, with some greenish-
black markings and black legs.
Male and female are similar,
though the female has a black
line and patterns along the
abdomen. Young insects have
yellowish-green in place of the
red. Could be confused only
with the Small Red Damselfly,
which is smaller, rarer, and
has red legs. Flight period
usually from late April
throughout the summer. Pairs
can often be seen mating; egg-
laying follows whilst they are
still paired. Common around
sheltered ponds almost
everywhere.

Common Blue Damselfly
Enallagma cyathigerum Robust,
medium-sized species of
damselfly, about 3cm long.
Male is pale blue with
interrupted black markings
along the abdomen, including
a distinctive 'stalked ball' on
the second segment from the
thorax; female is duller, more
greenish in colour. Adults can
be seen in flight from mid-
May through the summer,
often in abundance in
midsummer when they fly
low over the water in swarms.
Mating usually takes place
near the bank, then the pair
separates for the female to
submerge and lay eggs alone.
Common around ponds and
other water bodies throughout
the area.

Dragonflies

Southern Hawker *Aeshna cyanea* This large and conspicuous dragonfly is up to about 12cm long. Male has a blackish basic colour, strongly marked with paired greenish rounded triangles, except for the last few segments of the abdomen where they become blue and merge into one blotch; female is similar but all marks are greenish. A strong-flying insect that can travel long distances, it is on the wing from June–October. Despite its size and strong flight, it is harmless, though predatory on flying insects. Readily finds garden ponds, where the female lays eggs into surrounding vegetation or wet stonework. Common throughout.

Broad-bodied Chaser *Libellula depressa* Large bulky dragonfly, about 3-4cm long, with a broad heavy abdomen. Male becomes bright blue as it matures, with yellowish marks on the sides and large black patches at the base of all 4 wings; female and young males are similar but yellowish-brown. An early species, it appears from late April until July–August. It is a strong-flying insect that soon finds new sites, where the males will become aggressively territorial, driving away other males. A common and widespread species around ponds, except very small ones, throughout the area except in the far north.

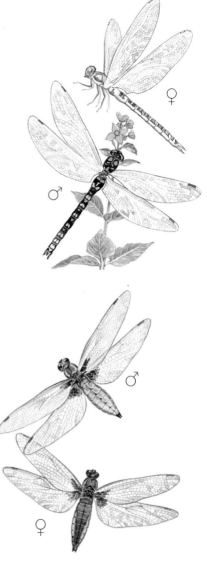

Butterflies

Small Tortoiseshell *Aglais urticae* A distinctive medium-sized butterfly with a wingspan of 5-6cm. Male and female are similar, with reddish-orange wings, marked with brown and yellow, and edged with a line of blue crescents. Can be seen at almost any time of year, as the adults hibernate, occasionally emerging on warm days or when disturbed. The eggs are laid on Stinging Nettles in sunny places, and these then hatch to produce clusters of yellowish-black spiny caterpillars. Common everywhere, wandering widely and becoming particularly abundant in late summer before hibernation.

Peacock *Inachis io* Large and striking butterfly with a wingspan of 6-7cm. Male and female are similar. The wings are a deep reddish-brown, edged with a greyish border, and all 4 are marked with a large 'peacock eye'; the undersides, visible when the butterfly closes its wings, are dull brown, mottled like tree bark. Like the Small Tortoiseshell, the adults hibernate, and may be seen at almost any time. Eggs are laid on Nettles, hatching into spiny caterpillars, rather like those of Small Tortoiseshell, but larger (up to 4.5cm) and blacker. Common and mobile throughout the area except in the far north.

Red Admiral *Vanessa atalanta*
Large and easily recognisable
butterfly with a wingspan of
up to 7.5cm. Male and female
are similar, though the male is
slightly smaller. The wings
are velvety-black, marked
with a diagonal band of red or
orange and patches of white;
the underside of the forewing
is similar, but is usually
concealed beneath the dull
brown underwing when the
wings are folded. Eggs are laid
singly on Nettles, producing
solitary spiny caterpillars. In
northern Europe, including
Britain, the insects are
migrants only, with most
failing to survive the winter;
they can be seen from March
–November.

Painted Lady *Cynthia cardui*
A large butterfly with a
wingspan of 6-7cm. The sexes
are similar, though the male is
slightly smaller, and are
tawny-orange to pinkish,
strongly marked with black
and white, especially at the
tips of the forewings; the
forewing underside is similar
but paler, while the hindwing
is strongly lined and mottled;
old insects may be very sun-
bleached. Eggs are laid singly,
most commonly on Thistles,
where the spiny black and
yellow caterpillar eventually
makes itself a web tent.
Migrates northwards from
North Africa and south
Europe, occurring variably in
the north from March–
October.

Butterflies

Comma *Polygonia c-album*
A deeply jagged wing edge distinguishes this medium-sized butterfly, which has a wingspan of 5-6cm. Male and female are similar, with tawny-orange wings above, marked with black and brown: the undersides are duller, mottled brownish-orange, but with the characteristic white 'comma' on the hindwing. The eggs are laid singly on Stinging Nettle, Hop or Elm leaves, and develop into brown and white caterpillars that resemble bird droppings. Commas are mobile and partly migratory, occurring widely through much of Europe except the far north, and are common in southern Britain.

Holly Blue *Celastrina argiolus*
Small attractive butterfly with a wingspan of about 3.5cm. Male and female are similar, with blue upperwings, though the female has more black towards the tips; the undersides are clear pale blue with black dots. Often seen around shrubs in spring and late summer. The Holly Blue is unusual in having 2 separate foodplants for different generations; eggs are laid on Holly in spring, then the females from that generation lay on Ivy, or occasionally other shrubs. The caterpillars from both generations are green and rather slug-like. This is the commonest blue garden butterfly.

Large White *Pieris brassicae*
Unpopular as one of the two
'Cabbage White' butterflies
that are such frequent garden
pests. Large, with a wingspan
of 6–7cm. Male and female are
roughly similar, both having
mainly white upperwings,
edged with black, though the
female has 2 black spots on
each forewing; the under-
wings are pale unmarked
yellowish-grey. Flies
throughout the summer. The
yellow eggs are laid in large
batches on Cabbages and
related plants, hatching out
into a mass of mottled
greyish-green caterpillars that
smell unpleasant. An
abundant and mobile insect,
with resident numbers
regularly swollen by
immigrants.

Small White *Pieris rapae* A
medium-sized white butterfly
with a wingspan of 4.5–5cm.
Male and female are broadly
similar, with white
upperwings variably marked
with black, though the female
usually has 2 black dots on the
forewing, the male only 1; the
undersides are yellowish, with
the hindwing unmarked and
the forewing black-spotted.
On the wing from April–
October. The eggs are laid
singly on the leaves of
Cabbages, and related plants,
both garden and wild, and
they hatch into green
caterpillars. An abundant
species throughout the area,
except in the extreme north.

Butterflies

Green-veined White *Pieris napi*
Medium-sized white butterfly
with a wingspan of about 5cm.
Similar to the Small White,
differing mainly in the
undersides of the wings,
which have broad greyish-
green stripes along most of
the veins, especially in the
spring generation; the
summer generation has paler
underwings, but the upper
forewing is more strongly
marked in black. Flies from
April–September. Eggs are
laid singly on wild species of
the Cabbage family, such as
Lady's Smock or Garlic
Mustard, but it is never a pest
of cultivated Brassicas. Mobile
and widespread, regularly
visiting gardens.

Black-veined White *Aporia
crataegi* A large butterfly with
a wingspan of 7cm or more.
Male and female are similar,
with white wings strongly
marked with thin black lines,
though the veining is rather
browner in the female. Flies
from May–July. Eggs are laid
in clusters on the leaves of
Hawthorn and other Rose
family shrubs, hatching into
bristly black, white and red
caterpillars which live in web
nests. Common over most of
Europe (but not Britain) in
scrub and grassy areas, not
infrequently entering gardens,
and occasionally a pest of
orchard crops.

Orange-tip *Anthocharis cardamines* This small to medium-sized butterfly has a wingspan of 4-5cm. The male is very distinctive, mainly white above but with the forewings strongly tipped with orange and a little black; the female lacks the orange, but both sexes have attractive marbled green and white underwings. Flies through spring and early summer. The eggs are laid singly close to the flowers of Lady's Smock and Garlic Mustard, hatching into long, thin, smooth caterpillars that eventually become green. The Orange-tip is common and widespread wherever its foodplants occur, frequently visiting, and occasionally breeding in, gardens.

Brimstone *Gonepteryx rhamni* One of the first heralds of spring; a medium-large butterfly with a wingspan of about 6cm. The male is a conspicuous clear yellow above and below, each wing having a small spot and a distinctive hook-tip; female similar in shape, but much paler, tinged greenish. Adults hibernate, emerging early in spring on warm days, flying widely in search of mates or foodplants; the second generation appears in July or August. The eggs are laid singly on the leaves of Buckthorn, and hatch into long, thin, greenish caterpillars with a white stripe. A frequent visitor to gardens throughout the area, except in the far north.

Moths

Poplar Hawkmoth *Laothoe populi* Large, well-camouflaged moth with a wingspan of 7–9cm. Male and female are similar, though the male is generally smaller, with marbled brownish-grey wings, occasionally pinkish, and orange-red patches at the base of the hindwings. Flies at night from July–October. The caterpillars are large and impressive, up to 6cm long, green with diagonal stripes, with the spike on the 8th segment that is a feature of most hawkmoth larvae; they feed on the leaves of Poplars and Willows. Common in gardens and parks wherever the foodplants occur.

Eyed Hawkmoth *Smerinthus ocellata* A large moth with a wingspan of 7–9cm. The uppersides of the forewings are marbled brownish; underwings are orange-pink, with striking blue and grey 'eyes'. The moth rests with the underwings hidden, flashing them, if disturbed, to frighten predators. Flies at night from May throughout the summer, in 2 generations. The caterpillar is similar to that of the Poplar Hawkmoth, and feeds on the leaves of Apple and Sallow, usually upside down. Frequent throughout most of Europe.

Privet Hawkmoth *Sphinx ligustri* A very large moth, with a wingspan of 10-12cm. The uppersides of the forewings are marbled and streaked brown, and the underwings are banded with pink and brown; the body is strongly striped with pink and dark brown. At rest, the wings tend to be closed along the body, in a roof-like shape. Flies at night in June and July. The caterpillars are very large, green, with strongly marked diagonal brown and white stripes, feeding mainly on Privet, less commonly on Lilac and Ash. Widespread throughout except in the north, though rarely common.

Hummingbird Hawkmoth *Macroglossum stellatarum* This little hawkmoth has a wingspan of 5-6cm. The uppersides of the forewings are brownish, striped darker, while the underwings are orange-yellow; the body is short and furry. This moth flies during the day, and has the distinctive habit of hovering in front of flowers, such as Honeysuckle or Valerian, to feed. Most commonly seen from April–August, often visiting gardens for the nectar flowers. The caterpillars feed on Bedstraws. In Britain, and other parts of north Europe, it is a migrant only.

Elephant Hawkmoth *Deilephila elpenor* A very distinctive medium-sized moth with a wingspan of about 6.5-7cm. Male and female are similar; both have forewings of bronze-green striped with pink, and pink and black hindwings; the body is pale brown striped with pink. The adults fly from evening into the night, during May–July, often visiting Honeysuckle and Rhododendron. Caterpillars feed on Willowherbs or garden *Clarkia*, eventually reaching about 8cm long, greyish-brown, with a horn at one end and eye-spots at the other.

Pale Tussock *Calliteara pudibunda* A medium-sized moth with a wingspan of about 4-5cm. Both male and female are undistinguished, greyish-white, hairy, banded with pale brown. They fly at night through May and June (when they may be attracted to lights). The caterpillars, in contrast to the adults, are very distinctive, being yellowish or green, with numerous long hairs, including 4 brushes of yellow hair and one tuft of orange hair. They feed on most native deciduous trees, such as Oak and Birch, and occur from July–September. Common throughout the area except in the far north.

Puss Moth *Cerura vinula*
Largish moth, with a
wingspan of 6–7cm. The adults
are similar, with silvery-grey
wings marked and striped
darker, and a silver-grey
fluffily hairy body. They fly at
night from May–July. The
caterpillar is extraordinary,
large and green, up to 7cm
long, with a reddish 'face',
darker camouflage markings
and 2 long striped tails; not
easily confused with any other
species. It feeds on Willows
and Poplars from July –
September. Reasonably
common and widespread
almost throughout, in parks
and gardens with suitable
trees.

Garden Tiger *Arctia caja*
Brightly coloured moth with a
wingspan of 5–7cm. Male and
female are similar, though the
male is slightly smaller; both
have forewings boldly marked
with brown and white, and
underwings that are orange
and black. On the wing at
night during July and August,
occasionally being attracted to
lights. The caterpillars are
conspicuous and familiar as
'woolly bears', reddish-brown
and black with numerous long
hairs; they feed on a wide
range of herbaceous plants
such as Docks and Stinging
Nettles, and can be found
from September through to
June. Common throughout
the area.

Moths

Cinnabar Moth *Tyria jacobaeae*
A rather small moth with a
wingspan of about 4cm. The
forewings are greyish-black,
marked with a red stripe and 2
dots; the underwings are
bright red, edged with black
— a distinctive combination.
On the wing from May–
August, mainly at night, but
often seen during the day.
The caterpillars are also
highly distinctive for their
combination of bright yellow-
orange with black rings — a
warning to predators that
they are distasteful; they feed
on Ragwort and its relatives
through July and August.
Common throughout the
area, except in the far north.

Sycamore Moth *Acronicta aceris*
Medium to small moth with a
wingspan of 4-4.5cm. The
forewings are greyish or
brown, marbled with white,
and the underwings are white
veined with grey-brown. Flies
at night from June–
September. The caterpillars
are much more distinctive
than the adults, with long
yellow and orange hairs, and a
line of black-edged white dots
along the back; they feed on
Sycamore, Maple, Horse
Chestnut and other trees
through August and
September. Common and
widespread wherever suitable
trees occur, except in the
north.

Large Yellow Underwing
Noctua pronuba A medium-sized
moth with a wingspan of 5-
5.5cm. The forewings are dull
mottled brown or yellowish.
The hindwings are bright
yellow-orange with a brown
border; they are flashed in
flight, and if the insect is
disturbed, to momentarily
confuse predators. Flies at
night from July–September,
often attracted to light. The
caterpillars are brown or
greenish, with rows of
tapering short dark stripes,
and they feed on many
different herbaceous plants
throughout the winter. A
common and widespread
species, with resident
populations regularly swollen
by populations from the
south.

Red Underwing *Catocala nupta*
A large moth with a wingspan
of 7-8cm. The forewings are
attractively marbled and
marked in browns and greys,
sometimes with a pink tinge.
The underwings are bright
red, banded with black; these
are flashed when the moth is
disturbed, or taking evasive
flight, to unsettle predators.
On the wing at night from
August–October. The
caterpillars are long and thin,
varying from yellow to grey,
with a fringe of hairs that
allows them to blend with
twigs when stretched out, and
several bud-like outgrowths.
They feed from May–July on
Willows and Poplars.
Common except in the north.

Moths

Silver Y *Autographa gamma*
Variably marked small-medium moth with a wingspan of 3.5-4cm. The wings are usually marbled and streaked brown, grey and white on the forewings, with a distinctive white 'Y' in the middle; the hindwings are greyish with a dark border. Often flies by day as well as by night, visiting flowers for nectar. The caterpillars are green and smooth, found on a wide range of herbaceous plants through the latter part of summer and into the autumn. This is a migrant species, moving northwards into most of Europe, where it breeds but does not overwinter.

Magpie Moth *Abraxas grossulariata* A small-medium moth with a wingspan of 3.5-4.5cm. The wings are white, blotched and spotted with black and yellow in a variable pattern, but always easily recognisable. The caterpillars are striped in similar colours, and they feed on Currants and Gooseberries (often becoming a pest), Plum, Apple and other shrubs. Both adults and caterpillars are highly unpalatable, and their bright colours serve as a warning. Adults fly at night during July and August, while the caterpillars live from September through to June. Common throughout the area, except in the far north.

Winter Moth *Operophtera brumata* A small moth, with a marked difference between the sexes. The male has a wingspan of 3-4cm, lightly marked with brown and yellow; the female, however, is virtually wingless, and incapable of flight, crawling up the trunks of fruit trees to lay eggs in the buds. The adults are about through the winter, from November–March, and the caterpillars feed on the leaves through April and May. The species is common almost throughout the area, sometimes becoming a pest of fruit trees, but controlled by grease bands to stop the females crawling up.

White Plume Moth *Pterophorus pentadactyla* One of the largest of the so-called micromoths, though it has a wingspan of only about 3cm. The species is distinctive for its white wings, which are feathered into 5 plumes at the tips, and its white legs, on which there are several projections. On the wing at night from May–August, frequently being attracted to light. The caterpillars are green and yellow, with tufts of hair, and they feed in rolled-up leaves of Bindweed. Common in gardens virtually throughout the area.

Grasshoppers

Common Field Grasshopper
Chorthippus brunneus A medium-large grasshopper, reaching about 3cm when mature. It is very variable in colour, most commonly brown, green or grey, with wings that are longer than the body. The short antennae help to distinguish the species from the bush-crickets. Younger stages are simply smaller versions, with shorter wings. The call of this species is a brief burst of sound, repeated irregularly. The adults occur from June to early autumn, and are frequent in rougher gardens, especially where there are dry, bare areas.

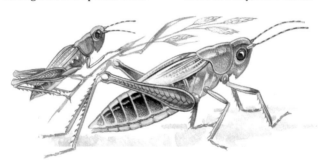

Meadow Grasshopper
Chorthippus parallelus A small-medium grasshopper, though the female is noticeably larger than the male, reaching about 3cm. Colour varies from green to brown or occasionally purplish. The species is unusual in that even mature adults have very short wings, which they are unable to use for flight. The call sounds rather like an old-fashioned sewing machine, given in bursts of about 3 seconds, repeated regularly. Adults are evident from June through to early autumn. Very common in grassland throughout the area, and occurring in gardens where there is longer grass, especially if slightly damp.

Speckled Bush-cricket
Leptophyes punctatissima A
medium-sized bush-cricket
with a body length of up to
2cm and antennae that are up
to 2-3 times this length. The
body is green, rather fat,
dotted all over with red or
white; the wings are very
short in both sexes (they are
flightless), and the female has
a long curved dagger-like
ovipositor (as do most female
bush-crickets). The scratchy
call is virtually inaudible.
Common in gardens where
there is dense vegetation, but
mainly southern in
distribution. May appear in
houses, attracted by light.

Oak Bush-cricket *Meconema
thalassinum* Small, slender
bush-cricket with a body
length of about 1.5cm. Both
sexes are green, with body-
length wings that allow them
to fly, albeit weakly; the
antennae are very long. The
male has a pair of claspers at
the rear end, while the female
has a dagger-like ovipositor
about 1cm long. The only call
is caused by the male
'drumming' on leaves with his
feet, but this is very faint.
Adults occur from July well
into autumn in areas where
there are deciduous trees,
from which they may fly to
lights. Common in southern
areas, absent in the north.

Crickets

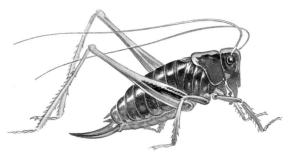

Dark Bush-cricket *Pholidoptera griseoaptera* A large and bulky bush-cricket with a body length of up to 3cm and antennae at least twice that length. The sexes are roughly similar, both essentially brown, but the male is smaller and often darker, while the female has long slightly curved ovipositors. Neither has well-developed wings, and they are unable to fly. The call is a short sharp burst, most commonly produced from late afternoon through into the night. Common in shrubberies and hedges throughout the area, except in the north.

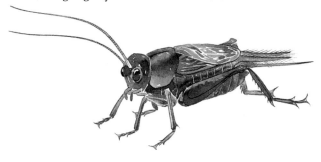

House Cricket *Acheta domesticus* A small cricket with a body length of 1.5-2cm. Similar to the bush-crickets, but more flattened, the species is brown, with well-developed wings and antennae that are rather longer than the body. The call is a bird-like chirp (often mistaken for a bird), emitted mainly in the evening or through the night. Although native to Asia, it is now frequent in houses, some gardens and rubbish-tips throughout much of Europe, but only abundant in warmer parts.

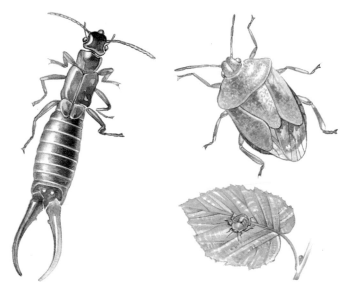

Common Earwig *Forficula auricularia* This insect is about 1-1.5cm long, shiny brown, with yellowish wing-cases that partly hide the wings, and a pair of brown pincers at the tip of the abdomen; the latter are strongly curved in the male, almost straight in the female. The species is mainly nocturnal, emerging from a daytime hiding-place to feed on flowers and fruit, often in large numbers. The female is unusual in that she guards her young until they can fend for themselves. It is much the commonest of a number of similar species, to be found almost everywhere.

Green Shield Bug *Palomena prasina* A characteristically shield-shaped bug, reaching about 1-1.5cm in length when fully mature. Wholly green in colour, apart from the brown tips to the wings. The younger stages are smaller, rounder and completely green, apart from when they first emerge from the eggs, when they are brown. The adults live in hedges and shrubby areas, overwintering (when they turn browner), then emerging to mate and lay eggs. They feed on plants, but are not normally a pest, though they are common almost throughout the area.

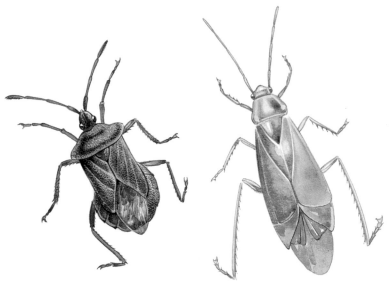

Squash Bug *Coreus marginatus*
A largish bug, 1-1.5cm long, brown all over except for the membranous part of the wings. It has long 4-segmented antennae, with 2 tiny horns on the head between them. The adult overwinters, emerging in spring to breed and lay; as with most bugs, the eggs hatch into miniature replicas of the adults, which pass through a number of similar stages before becoming fully mature. The foodplants are Docks and Sorrels or, most frequently in gardens, Rhubarb, which is related to Docks. Common in southern areas, but absent from the north.

Common Green Capsid
Lygocoris pabulinus A smallish bug, usually under 1cm long. The adults are green, apart from the brown membranous wing-tips; younger generations are almost wholly green. Eggs are laid in September on shrubby plants, especially fruits such as Raspberries; these remain overwinter, then the emerging young feed on the developing leaves, before moving to herbaceous plants. A second generation is produced which then lays the overwintering eggs again. A common and widespread species, occasionally becoming a minor pest.

Common Pond Skater *Gerris lacustris* Conspicuous medium-sized bug, about 1cm long, readily recognised through its distinctive habit of 'skating' around on the water-surface, using a rowing type of movement. Brownish in colour. A scavenger on anything that lands on the water surface, alive or dead. The adults can fly well, and move away from water to hibernate through the winter, returning in spring to lay their eggs. These hatch into nymphs that gradually enlarge to become adults by July. A common and widespread insect, though there are a number of similar species.

Common Backswimmer *Notonecta glauca* A largish water bug, reaching 1.5cm in length. Backswimmers are very distinctive as a group for their habit of swimming upside down in the water, usually close to the surface. They are voracious predators, attacking tadpoles, young fishes and anything of a similar size. Adults mate in late winter or early spring, the eggs being laid shortly afterwards into the stems of water-plants; these hatch into nymphs, which grow into adults over a period of about 2 months. This species is a common visitor to garden ponds throughout the area, readily flying and finding new sites.

Common Froghopper *Philaenus spumarius* Also known as 'cuckoo-spit' from the frothy substance produced by the developing nymph that feeds on plant juices, then secretes the froth to hide and protect itself. The nymph may move several times, leaving froth behind, before maturing into a small brownish froghopper that is about 3-4mm long. The adults are about from June to late autumn, when the females lay eggs into crevices in stems, from which the new nymphs will hatch in the following spring. They are common throughout the area on soft herbaceous plants.

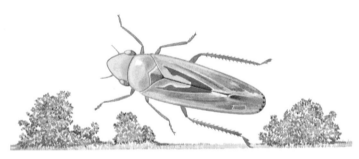

Rhododendron Leafhopper
Graphocephala fennahi
Surprisingly conspicuous bug, though only 4-7mm long. The adults, which often occur in large numbers, are brightly green and red-striped. Both adults and nymphs feed on Rhododendrons, and they may carry an infection known as bud blast, so they are rarely welcome in gardens. Adults are visible from May–October. The species is North American in origin, but was introduced to Britain with imported plant material in the 1930s, and is now common throughout the south.

Woolly Aphid *Eriosoma lanigerum* The white woolly and rather waxy substance often found in the crevices of tree bark conceals colonies of this aphid. The insects themselves are very small, purplish black, but wholly concealed by the masses of fluff. The wingless female overwinters in crevices, then produces a succession of generations through the summer, including some winged insects which will spread the population. It is most common on Apple trees, where some damage and swelling may be caused, though it is rarely a serious pest. Common throughout the area.

Blackfly *Aphis fabae* This small black aphid, also known as the Black Bean Aphid, is a common and familiar garden pest. The life-cycle is complex: in late summer, winged females move from beans or other host plants to shrubs such as Spindle, where wingless females are produced; winged males mate with these, who then lay eggs. In spring, the eggs hatch into wingless females which produce live young, and ultimately winged insects which then return to the herbaceous host in the summer. Abundant almost throughout, except in the coldest or wettest areas.

Bugs

Rose Aphid *Macrosiphum rosae*
A relatively large aphid, 2–3mm long, readily visible on the undersides of leaves. The insect is green or pink, with 2 long black cornicles (tubes) near the rear end (which help to distinguish it from similar rose-inhabiting species). Occurs in abundance on Roses in the spring and early summer (or longer if pruning produces new growth), then the second generation is produced on Teasels and Scabious relatives in late summer. Overwinters as eggs. A common and widespread species virtually throughout.

Cabbage Whitefly *Aleyrodes proletella* Tiny insect, with a wingspan of about 3mm. Although a bug (and therefore related to aphids) it closely resembles a tiny moth in form. The body and wings are waxy-white. It occurs in large colonies on the undersides of plants. There are several similar species, but they can usually be distinguished by their host plant, i.e. Cabbage Whitefly normally occurs only on Cabbage. Breeding is continual throughout the summer so that by autumn there are large numbers, which may damage and discolour the host plant. A widespread and common species.

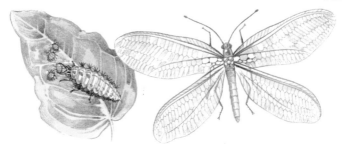

Green Lacewing *Chrysopa 7-punctata* A conspicuous insect, 3–4cm long. The body is bright green and the transparent green-veined wings are held in a roof-like position along its length. The eyes are metallic. The yellowish eggs are laid at the ends of long stalks fastened to the undersides of leaves; these then hatch into highly carnivorous larvae (which may eat all the unhatched eggs) which prey on aphids and other small invertebrates. The adults are also predatory; they fly at night, mainly in summer and autumn, but some overwinter. They are common around gardens, and often come into houses.

Crane-fly *Tipula paludosa* One of the largest flies, with a body length of 2.5–3cm. Also known as 'Daddy Long-legs' because of its habit of trailing its long legs behind it in flight. The body is greyish-brown and the wings are translucently brown. Adults fly throughout the spring and summer, becoming most abundant by August–September. The larvae (known as, 'leather-jackets') develop in large numbers in the soil under lawns and pasture, sometimes causing considerable damage. A common and widespread species, though there are many other similar ones.

Flies

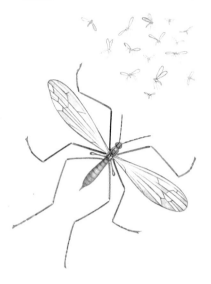

Winter Gnat *Trichocera relegationis* Resembles a small Crane-fly, with a body length of about 1cm. The body is greyish-brown in colour and the wings are transparent greyish-brown. Frequently occurs in small swarms; the name derives from the insect's regular appearance even on the coldest days of winter, though it also occurs at other times. The larvae feed in rotting wood and leaves, and the adults are completely harmless, though occasionally mistaken for mosquitoes. Common and widespread throughout the area.

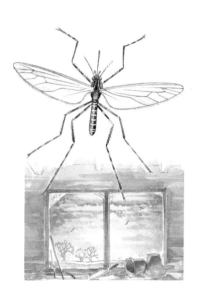

Mosquito *Culiseta annulata* One of the more distinctive amongst the commoner species of mosquitoes. It has a body length of 6-7mm, and both body and legs are strongly white-banded, while the wings are distinctively spotted. As with other mosquitoes, it is only the female which bites, and the harmless male can be distinguished by his branched feathery antennae. This species passes the winter as an adult, often in outbuildings, from which it may emerge to feed on warmer winter days. A common and widespread species throughout the area.

Poecilobothrus nobilitatus
Although very small (4–5mm long), and not well known enough to merit an English name, this fly is surprisingly conspicuous. It has a metallic green body, red eyes, and smoky wings which, in the male, are white-tipped. It occurs in large swarms on mud or at the edge of ponds (including garden ones), where there will be much activity and wing-waving as males court females and fight other males. It is a common species throughout the area, in suitable habitats, except in the north.

Hoverfly *Syrphus ribesii*
Although many of them are very distinctive, few of the hundreds of hoverflies have distinct English names. This species is relatively large, with a body length of 1–1.5cm; the thorax is black with brown hair, and the abdomen is strongly marked with yellow stripes on black (looking slightly wasp-like, but smaller, not 'waisted', and with only 2 wings). The adults occur throughout the summer, often in abundance, visiting flowers for nectar. The larvae are rather like small slugs, and are predatory on aphids. Widespread and common throughout.

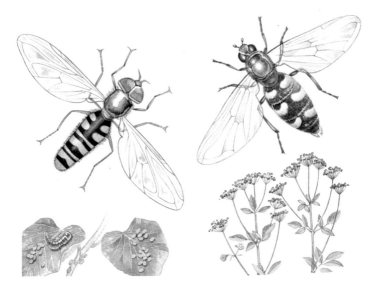

Hoverfly *Episyrphus balteatus*
One of the commonest of
hoverflies. This species is
rather smaller than *Syrphus
ribesii*, with a body length of
about 1cm, and slender. The
thorax is black with brown
hairs, and the abdomen is
yellow marked with a series of
broad then narrow lines. The
adults visit flowers in
abundance, and in some years
the resident populations are
swollen by large numbers of
immigrants moving
northwards from southern
Europe. The larvae are slug-
like and feed on aphids.
Common and widespread
throughout the area.

Hoverfly *Scaeva pyrastri* A large
hoverfly, with a broad body
up to 1.6cm long. The eyes are
maroon, the thorax is black
with brown hairs, and the
abdomen is black with 3 pairs
of broad white or cream
curved stripes, though
occasional all-black individuals
occur. The adults are
abundant from June until
autumn, with resident
numbers swollen by
immigrants from the south in
certain years; they are most
commonly seen at flowers.
The larvae are predatory,
feeding mainly on aphids. A
common species, widespread
throughout the area.

Narcissus-fly *Merodon equestris*
A medium to large hoverfly, up to about 1.4cm long. Brown, hairy and variable in colour, it resembles some smaller Bumble Bees in form. The male flies low and hovers in suitable grassy areas awaiting the female; after mating, the female lays her eggs at the base of bulbous plants, such as Bluebells and Daffodils. The larvae then burrow into the bulbous base of the plant and feed on it; they can be a minor pest in areas where bulbs are important. Adults are on the wing from early spring until late summer, and they are common throughout.

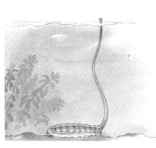

Drone-fly *Eristalis tenax* A medium-sized hoverfly with a body length of 1.2–1.4cm. This fly strongly resembles the male Honey Bee (hence the common name), though it has 2 wings not 4. The adults hover frequently (much more than bees) and are numerous in sunny sheltered areas, especially where flowers are abundant. The eggs are laid near stagnant water or farmyard manure heaps, into which the larvae migrate, becoming known as 'rat-tailed maggots' due to their extendable breathing tubes. This is a very common and widespread species, though there are also several other similar ones.

Flies

Holly Leaf-miner *Phytomyza ilicis* The fly itself is tiny (2–3mm long) and rarely noticed. However, it lays its eggs close to the base of the midrib of young Holly leaves in the spring. When the larva hatches, it feeds between the upper and lower layers of the leaf, leaving a mined trail that gradually enlarges as the larva grows. The affected leaves are very conspicuous and can be seen at all seasons, though the larva may have long departed. An abundant and widespread insect, occurring throughout Europe.

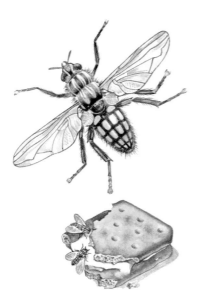

Flesh-fly *Sarcophaga carnaria* A large fly with a body length of about 1.5cm. It is grey to black, with a striped thorax and a spotted or chequered abdomen, both segments being very bristly. The feet are noticeably large. The life-cycle is unusual in that the fertilised eggs hatch within the female, and the larvae are laid directly into suitable rotting meat or other food; the larvae produce digestive enzymes, and prevent themselves from drowning in the resultant liquid by maintaining air holes. Common and widespread throughout the area.

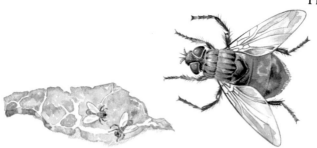

Bluebottle *Calliphora vomitoria*
A distinctive medium-sized fly, about 1cm long. The abdomen is metallic blue and hairy (there are several very similar species to which the common name is also given). The adults can occur at all times of year, except in very cold areas, readily coming inside. The eggs are laid in meat, with any available food being found very quickly; the white larvae are typical 'maggots'. The male feeds mainly at flowers. An abundant and very widespread species, occurring wherever there is suitable food.

Greenbottle *Lucilia caesar*
Similar in general form to the Bluebottle, but with a strikingly metallic green body, which is rather less obscured by hairs. The green colour may gradually change to reddish-copper as the insect ages. Although the life-cycle is similar to that of the Bluebottle, Greenbottles tend to lay their eggs mainly in rotting carcases, not visiting houses so readily. The male spends most of his time feeding at flowers, or basking in the sun. Common and widespread throughout the area (though the common name refers to several very similar species).

Cluster-fly *Pollenia rudis* A medium-small fly, about 7–9mm long, with a chequered abdomen and golden-brown hairs on the thorax. Adults can occur in almost any month, though largest numbers are likely to be seen in spring or autumn (or at a hibernation site). Large numbers gather in autumn to enter house-lofts or other suitable overwintering sites, and dozy flies may often enter the living area from here during the winter. The larvae are parasites of earthworms and possibly of other invertebrates. Widespread and common throughout the area.

Common House-fly *Musca domestica* Familiar worldwide, with its close association with man; a small fly, 8–9mm long, greyish with orange-buff on the abdomen. May be seen in any month in warmer parts of Europe, but is most common from June–October. Eggs are laid in rotting material of various sorts and, in warm conditions, these may become new adult flies within about a week. The Face-fly, *Musca autumnalis*, is very similar, but a little more dumpy, with more orange on the abdomen. Both species are abundant and widespread throughout the area.

Noon-fly *Mesembrina meridiana*
A medium-large fly with a
body length of 1.3-1.5cm. The
body is blackish and hairy —
like that of many other flies —
but this species can be
distinguished from most by
the orange suffusion at the
base of the wings, which is
readily visible. The adults visit
flowers, especially Umbellifers
such as Angelica, for nectar,
and are often seen sunbathing
in clusters on walls or tree-
trunks. The larvae feed on
decaying matter. A common
and widespread species,
occurring in gardens and
other habitats throughout the
area.

Gooseberry Sawfly *Nematus
ribesii* A medium-sized sawfly
with a body varying in length
from 0.6-1.1cm, the female
generally being the larger.
The female is brownish-
yellow, while the male is
partly marked with black. The
caterpillars are more familiar,
often occurring abundantly on
Gooseberry and Currant
bushes; they are pale
greenish-yellow, speckled
with black, and they can
rapidly strip their host plant
down to the leaf veins,
especially as numbers build up
through several generations
in a warm summer. Common
throughout the area, except in
the far north.

Garden Black Ant *Lasius niger*
A familiar species. The female
workers are black and
wingless, about 4mm long, and
it is these that forage
everywhere and regularly
enter houses in search of
food. On warm summer days,
winged females (queens) and
winged males emerge in vast
swarms to mate, after which
the males die and the queens
form new colonies. The queen
ants are up to about 1cm long.
The nests are built under
paving stones, in walls, or
other suitable dry areas, and
they are abundant almost
everywhere.

Parasitic Wasp *Apanteles
glomeratus* One of many
parasitic wasps. In this
particular species, the adults
are black and very small. They
lay up to 150 eggs at a time in
the caterpillars of Large White
Butterflies; these then hatch
into tiny larvae that gradually
eat their hosts. Parasitised
caterpillars may behave
erratically, and are often in
conspicuous places.
Eventually, the larvae emerge
and pupate in yellow cocoons
around the remains of the
caterpillar. The species is
common and widespread
virtually throughout the area,
wherever the host butterfly
occurs.

Yellow Ophion *Ophion luteus*
A large parasitic ichneumon-
fly with a body length of 1.5–
2cm and a wingspan of 3cm.
The body is yellowish-brown,
with the characteristic
'waisted' shape of the wasp-
relatives (Hymenoptera). The
adults appear in late summer,
lasting through the autumn.
They fly at night, and are
often attracted to lights,
coming into houses. The
female lays her eggs in the
caterpillars of various moths,
such as the Sycamore Moth,
which are then eaten by the
larvae. A common and
widespread species
throughout the area.

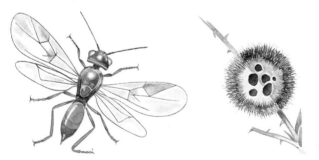

Rose Gall *Diplolepis eleganteriae*
The adult gall-wasps of this
species are tiny insects, about
3mm long, but the galls that
they cause are much more
conspicuous. In spring, the
mated female lays eggs into
the tissue on the underside of
a rose-leaf; as each larva
matures, it causes the
formation of a reddish pea-
like gall, which falls off in the
autumn, and the adults
emerge the following spring.
A related species, *Diplolepis
nervosus*, causes spiky galls, also
on Roses. Both are widespread
and reasonably common.

Wasps

Common Wasp *Vespula vulgaris*
This is the all-too-familiar wasp that visits houses and gardens for fruit and other sweet food. Wasps are colonial, with a single overwintered queen building up a papery nest in a hole, or under a shed, which may eventually enlarge to contain several thousand individuals. At first, the worker wasps collect insects to feed to the developing larvae; later in the summer, they simply feed themselves, on sweet substances, and it is then that they become a nuisance as they seek out fruit and jam. Abundant everywhere.

Hornet *Vespa crabro* A very large wasp-like insect with a body length of about 3cm; even the worker Hornets are larger than the queens of Common Wasps. The body is mainly banded yellow and red, with some black. Annual colonies are constructed in buildings or hollow trees, though the same site may be used several years running. It is a predator, like other members of the wasp family, but is generally docile despite its size and appearance. Not infrequently visits gardens. The species is most common in wooded southern areas, but can occur elsewhere.

Tawny Mining Bee *Andrena fulva* This attractive little bee has a yellowish-brown hairy body, about 1cm long, though the male is rather smaller and darker. The nest is a crater-like construction of fine soil, with a central hole, often seen in dry lawns — hence the alternative common name of Lawn Bee. The species is harmless, and does not sting humans, spending most of its time foraging for nectar on flowers such as Currants, and other garden plants, where it performs an important pollination service. Generally common and widespread, except in the north.

Leaf-cutter Bee *Megachile centuncularis* This insect resembles the Honey Bee, though it is rather hairier, and the female has orange hairs under the abdomen. However, they become noticeable because the female cuts almost circular discs from the leaves of Roses which she uses to build the cells of the nest. This is a fascinating process to watch, as the disc is rapidly cut and carried away, and the results can be commonly seen in garden Roses. The nest itself is usually in rotting wood. Common throughout the area, except in the far north.

Bees

Violet Carpenter Bee *Xylocopa violacea* The adult of this species is a highly conspicuous insect, hard to confuse with anything else. The body is large, about 2cm long, hairy and blackish-purple. The wings are a lovely blue-violet tint. It flies by day, constantly visiting flowers for nectar, and is on the wing most of the summer. Although it can sting, the species is generally quite harmless. The nest is a burrow excavated in wood, hence the common name. It is increasingly abundant southwards in Europe, occurring in Britain and other northern areas only as a rare vagrant.

Honey Bee *Apis mellifera* One of the most familiar of all insects. Worker bees are about 1cm long though the males and queens are rather larger. The body varies from orange-brown to black. Permanent colonies are located mainly in managed hives, but also occur in the wild in hollow trees or occasionally in the open, and may contain up to 50,000 bees. They perform a vital function of pollination as well as producing honey. The bulk of the population is made up of sterile females (workers), who do all the foraging. Males (drones) are slightly squatter, and less active, appearing in the summer. Queens are larger than either. Found throughout the area, except in the very coldest parts.

Flower Bee *Anthophora retusa*
A largish bee with a body length of 1.5cm or more, as broad and hairy as a Bumble Bee. However, it is blackish, and the female has conspicuous orange-haired pollen baskets on her hind legs. The male is rather less black, and has conspicuously hairy legs, but no pollen baskets. The bee is particularly noticeable in spring when foraging for pollen and nectar, often visiting garden flowers such as *Aubretia*. The nest is made in a hole in the ground, or a bank. This, or similar species, occurs throughout the area except in the far north.

Bumble Bee *Bombus pascuorum*
One of many species of Bumble Bees which are generally readily recognisable as a group but hard to distinguish as separate species. Such insects are large, with body lengths of 1.5–2.5cm, broad and very hairy, marked with a combination of black, brown, white and yellow. Some species are conspicuously orange-tailed. They occur in annual colonies, in holes in the ground, or under garden sheds, with numbers building up according to food supply and weather. Only the queen survives the winter, to found a new colony in the following spring. Common throughout as a group, with some species confined to specific areas.

Violet Ground Beetle *Carabus violaceus* A large and very active beetle with a body length of about 2.5cm. It is a rather slender insect, with dark blue-black wing-cases and a violet-edged thorax. At night, it is a voracious predator, attacking various insects and other invertebrates. During the day it hides under stones or logs, only moving if disturbed. The adults appear from June–August. The species passes the winter as a carnivorous larva. Common and widespread throughout the area, except in the far north.

Ground Beetle *Nebria brevicollis* A small ground beetle with a body length of about 1cm, or slightly more. The body and wing-cases are shiny black and the legs reddish-brown. Like most other ground beetles, it is a nocturnal predator, hiding under stones or wood during the day. May appear at virtually any time, but is most likely to be seen during April–June and August–October. The larvae are actively carnivorous. Generally common in gardens throughout except in the far north. There are many other ground beetles, which all tend to be fast-moving and nocturnal.

Sexton Beetle *Nicrophorus vespillo* A distinctive medium-sized beetle with a body length of about 2cm. The wing-cases are shiny black, conspicuously marked with orange-red transverse bands, which can hardly be confused with anything else. The adults gather at corpses of small creatures, which they bury by removing the soil from beneath them, even moving them to a better site if necessary. The eggs are then laid into chambers stocked with carrion, and the larvae eventually move to the corpse as they grow. Occurs throughout the area, except in the far north, though rarely very common.

 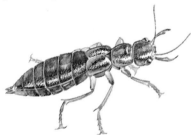

Devil's Coach-horse *Staphylinus olens* A long thin beetle with a body length of 2–3cm. It has a narrow black hairy body, with short wing-cases that leave most of the abdomen exposed, though the wings are full sized. If threatened, the beetle opens its impressive jaws, and raises its 'tail'. It is a nocturnal predator, hiding under stones and logs by day, and easily overlooked. The larva is also highly carnivorous. It is a common and widespread species in gardens and parks, except in the far north.

Beetles

Stag Beetle *Lucanus cervus*
A very large beetle, with the male reaching up to 6-7cm in length, though the female is smaller. Both sexes have black bodies with reddish-brown wing-cases, but the male has distinctive large 'antlers' (hence the common name) which are used for grappling with other males, though otherwise harmless. Feeds on sap. The large larvae live in rotting wood, taking several years to mature; the adults emerge in May or June, and can be seen until July, flying surprisingly well, on warm evenings. Not uncommon in gardens, but becoming rarer, and rare or absent from much of the north.

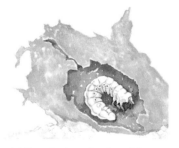

Lesser Stag Beetle *Dorcus parallelipipedus* Slightly smaller and more slender than a female Stag Beetle, with a body length of 3-4cm. The species is similar in appearance to the Stag Beetle but has dull black wing-cases, and the male has only small 'antlers'. A slow-moving creature, usually hiding during the day. Most commonly seen from April–October, though can be found in rotting wood right through the winter. The larvae live in dead wood and are quite easily attracted to garden wood piles. Common and wide-spread, except in the far north.

Dor Beetle *Geotrupes stercorarius*
A medium-large beetle with a
body length of about 2cm. The
body is shiny black above,
with ridged wing-cases, and
bluish below, with hairy legs.
This species is often badly
infested with mites, giving it
the alternative common name
of Lousy Watchman. Adults
fly well, mainly in the evening
or at night, and can be seen
from spring until autumn.
The larvae feed on dung,
usually from cows, but they
are regular visitors to
gardens. A common and
widespread species, occurring
throughout the area.

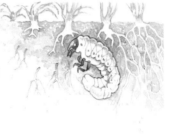

Cockchafer *Melolontha
melolontha* A medium-large
beetle with a broad body that
is 2-3cm long. The adult is
distinctive, with chestnut-
brown wing-cases (powdered
with white when the beetle is
newly emerged) and a hairy
abdomen; the male has
broadly feathered antennae.
Adults emerge in May (hence
their alternative name of May
Bug), when they are
sometimes abundant, often
crashing against windows at
night. The larvae live in the
soil and feed on plant roots,
occasionally becoming a pest.
Common and widespread
throughout the area, though
declining.

Beetles

Rose Chafer *Cetonia aurata* A beautiful medium-sized beetle with a body length of 2-3cm. The adult is bright metallic green, sometimes tinged with copper, and can hardly be mistaken for anything else, except for a few closely related but rarer species. Often visits flowers, including Roses as the name suggests, to feed, and is on the wing during the day, throughout the summer. The larvae live in dead wood, especially Willows and Poplars, or other rotting material. This species is widespread and moderately common throughout the area.

10-spot Ladybird *Adalia 10-punctata* A small beetle with a body length of 3-4mm. The adult is generally orangey-red with about 10 black spots (though the number is highly variable) and always has pale yellowish legs. It is visible by day through much of the year, from March until October. The larvae, like those of most ladybirds, are highly predatory; they feed mainly on aphids, a habit which makes them popular garden visitors. A common and widespread species, occurring throughout the year, though varying annually in abundance.

7-spot Ladybird *Coccinella 7-punctata* One of the commonest and most characteristic of the many ladybirds, with an oval body about 5-8mm long and bright red wing-cases with 7 black dots (though occasionally these vary in number); the legs are black. The 2-spot Ladybird, *Adalia bipunctata*, is similar, but has only two spots, and is rather smaller. Both species are visible by day, and the adults can be seen throughout the year, hibernating in groups on vegetation through the coldest period. The larvae are predatory on aphids and other slow-moving insects. Common throughout the area, though variable year to year.

Woodlouse *Oniscus asellus* One of the few land-dwelling crustaceans, reaching a body length of 1.5-2cm. It is greyish-brown in colour, usually with a paler 'fringe' surrounding the body, and sometimes marked with lighter spots. The young are miniature versions of adults slowly growing larger, so any colony will contain a wide variety of sizes. The female carries her young in a pouch below the body at first. Woodlice are mainly nocturnal, hiding under stones and wood by day, to avoid desiccation and predators. The species is common almost everywhere, especially in damp regions.

Crustaceans

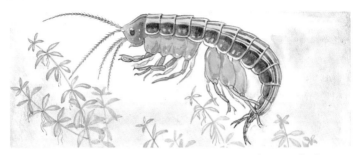

Freshwater Shrimp *Gammarus pulex* One of several freshwater 'shrimps' (not closely related to true shrimps), with a body length of about 2cm. The body is pale brown or greyish in colour, with a distinct curved shape. Although primarily an inhabitant of well-oxygenated waters such as streams, it can occur in garden ponds that have moving water, or are large and well-oxygenated by aquatic plants. Mainly feeds on rotting plant and animal material. Numbers become abundant in favourable conditions. Widespread almost throughout the area, though in Ireland it is introduced rather than native.

Pill Bug *Armadillidium vulgare* A type of woodlouse, with a body length of 1.5-2cm. It differs from the Common Woodlouse, and from many other species, by its ability to roll into a tight ball to escape predators. It is usually uniform grey, with well-defined body segments which allow it to roll up more easily. The Pill Bug is common around old walls, houses, and parts of gardens where there have been buildings, and is generally widespread throughout Europe.

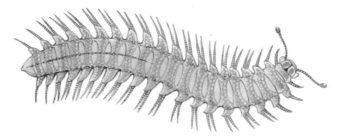

Millipede *Polydesmus angustus*
One of a large number of millipedes, this one has a body length of 2-2.5cm. It is narrow and flattened, not unlike the Centipede, but it generally differs from the latter in having 2 pairs of legs on most segments, and it is more sluggish, partly because it is not a predator. It feeds mainly on plant material, including garden plants, though rarely becomes a serious pest. This species is widespread over much of Europe, except the far north, east and south.

Centipede *Lithobius forficatus*
One of a number of related species, this one has a body length of about 2-3cm. Shiny brown in colour, the long body is clearly divided into about 15 segments, each of which bears a pair of legs. It is unlikely to have a hundred legs, though it is easy to see how the common name has arisen. It is a voracious and active predator, hiding under stones and logs by day, and emerging at night. Common and widespread in gardens and many other habitats throughout Europe.

Molluscs

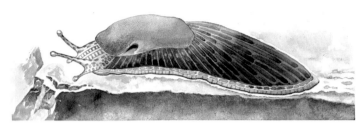

Black Slug *Arion ater* This very large slug reaches 10–15cm in length. Although highly variable in colour, size alone helps to distinguish it from other slugs. It is commonly black, but may be brown, grey or pale creamy-orange, and often has an orange skirt around the base of the body. The species is abundant in gardens (and many other habitats), wherever there is cover to hide during the day or in dry periods, and ample plant food to eat at night. Widespread throughout the area except in the far north.

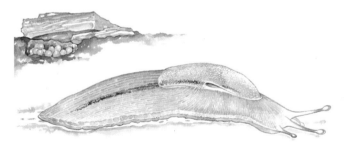

Garden Slug *Arion hortensis* A smallish slug, with a body length of 2–4cm. It is slender, typically streaked greyish or brownish above, with a dark band running around the body next to the orange-coloured underside. There is no external shell. The shiny white spherical eggs are laid under stones and logs; breeding continues almost throughout the year. The animal feeds on large amounts of plant material, with a particular fondness for soft vegetation such as seedlings, which makes it a serious pest in many gardens. It is common throughout the area.

Garden Snail *Helix aspersa*
A large, rounded snail with a shell that is about 3.5–4cm across in either direction. The shell is variable in colour, but is generally yellowish banded with brown. This is probably the commonest snail to be found in gardens and towns, occurring almost everywhere except in highly polluted districts. By day, it hides under stones or logs, emerging at night to feed on plant material. During hibernation it withdraws into the shell, sealing the entrance. Widespread, particularly in milder western and coastal areas.

Earthworm *Lumbricus terrestris*
Familiar cylindrical invertebrate, with a length of up to 10cm. The long, thin body is more pointed at one end than the other, and is brownish-red or greyish in colour, with an orange-red collar-like area (the clitellum) about halfway along. The role of Earthworms in helping to aerate and fertilise garden soils is well known, and they are abundant in most gardens. There are a number of similar species, all of which form the food of birds such as thrushes. Common and widespread throughout.

Spiders

Garden Spider *Araneus diadematus* One of the largest and most distinctive of garden spiders, with a body length of over 1cm, especially at full maturity in autumn. The female is larger and much more conspicuous than the male; the large rounded body is marked with a white-dotted cross. Size and apparent abundance increase through the summer, the spiders becoming extremely visible by autumn. The numerous large, near-circular orb webs hang from vegetation and sheds. A common and widespread species throughout the area.

Daddy Long-legs Spider *Pholcus phalangioides* This spider has an oval cylindrical body, 8–10mm long, with extremely long thin legs. It resembles the Harvestman, but can be distinguished by the 2-part body and its habit of making a web. It is greyish-brown, with yellow marks. The untidy web is spun in the corners of sheds and rooms where the spider sits upside-down waiting for prey. The species is also known as the Cellar Spider, indicating one of its preferred habitats. Common and widespread throughout the area, except in the far north.

Common House Spider
Tegenaria gigantea A large and
conspicuous spider with a
body length of up to 1.5cm and
long hairy legs. There are
several similar species, with
rather confused names, but
they can be identified as a
group by their brown bodies,
marked with a black herring-
bone pattern, their hairy legs,
and by being often seen away
from their webs. They can
move very fast, often causing
alarm when in confined
rooms. The large untidy webs
are built in the corners of
rooms or sheds, with a funnel
to which the spider can
retreat. Common throughout
the area.

Wolf Spider *Pisaura mirabilis*
One of several species of wolf
spiders, with a body length of
up to 1.5cm and long stout
legs. The body is greyish-
white, marked with darker
longitudinal stripes and
patterns. When the eggs are
laid, the female carries them,
in the form of a large white
ball, in her fangs; as they
begin to hatch, she attaches
the ball to a plant and covers
the area with a silken cocoon,
over which she stands guard.
At this stage, they become a
very visible species. Mainly
seen from May–August. Not
uncommon in gardens where
there is rough herbage.
Common throughout the
area.

Spiders/Harvestmen

Zebra Spider *Salticus scenicus*
Surprisingly noticeable spider, despite a body length of only 5-7mm. The oval body is black marked with white stripes (hence the common name) and the short legs are banded with black and white. It is a jumping spider, which builds no nest but stalks its prey and leaps onto it, often from a considerable distance. Favoured habitats are the sunny walls of sheds and houses, where the spider moves rapidly around in search of prey. Most often seen from May–September. It is common and widespread.

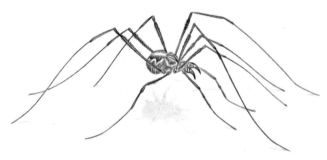

Harvestman *Phalangium opilio*
A spider-like creature with an oval body of 5-9mm long and extremely long slender legs. It is related to spiders, but the body, pale greyish and with a dark brown saddle-like marking on much of the upper surface, is not divided into 2 distinct parts. A scavenger and minor predator, the Harvestman is mainly nocturnal, but often seen during the day. Common throughout the area in many habitats, including gardens, especially where there is some rougher habitat.

Further Reading

Buczacki, S., *Ground Rules for Gardeners*. Collins, London, 1986.

Caplan, B. (Ed), *The Complete Manual of Organic Gardening*. Headline Publishing, London, 1992.

Chinery, M., *The Insects of Britain and Western Europe*. Collins, London, 1986.

Corbet, G. and Southern, H., *The Handbook of British Mammals*. Mammal Society/Blackwell Scientific, Oxford, 1977.

Fitter, R. and Manual, R., *Field Guide to Freshwater Life*. Collins, London, 1986.

Flegg, J., *The Green Guide to Birds*. New Holland, London, 1992.

Gardens of England and Wales Open to the Public. Published annually by the National Gardens Scheme (see Useful Addresses).

Gibbons, Bob and Liz, *Creating a Wildlife Garden*. Hamlyn, London, 1988.

Goodden, Robert and Rosemary, *The Green Guide to Butterflies*. New Holland, London, 1992.

Philip, C. and Lord, A., *The Plant Finder*. The Hardy Plant Society (see Useful Addresses), published regularly.

Useful Addresses

Hardy Plant Society
Lakeside, Gaines Road, Whitbourne, Worcs WR6 5RD. Publishers
of *The Plant Finder*.

Henry Doubleday Research Foundation
Ryton Organic Garden, Ryton-On-Dunsmore, Coventry CV8
3LG. Promotes various aspects of organic gardening.

National Gardens Scheme
57 Lower Belgrave Street, London SW1W 0LR. Publishes the
'Yellow Book' garden guide.

Royal Horticultural Society
Vincent Square, London SW1P 2PE.

Royal Society for Nature Conservation
The Green, Witham Park, Waterside South, Lincoln LN5 7JR.

Royal Society for the Protection of Birds
The Lodge, Sandy, Beds SG19 2DL.

Index

Index

Index

Index